NATHANIEL HAWTHORNE
(1804 – 1864)

# QUOTATIONS

OF

## *Nathaniel Hawthorne*

APPLEWOOD BOOKS
Carlisle, Massachusetts

Thank you for purchasing an Applewood book. Applewood reprints America's lively classics — books from the past that are still of interest to modern readers. For a free copy of our current catalog, please write or visit us at Applewood Books, 1 River Road, Carlisle, Massachusetts 01741.

www.awb.com

978-1-4290-9459-7

10 9 8 7 6 5 4 3 2

MANUFACTURED IN THE UNITED STATES OF AMERICA
WITH AMERICAN-MADE MATERIALS

# Nathaniel Hawthorne

NATHANIEL HAWTHORNE was born July 4, 1804, in Salem, Massachusetts. His sea captain father died less than four years later, leaving the family in financial difficulty. Funded by his mother's relations, Hawthorne attended Bowdoin College in Brunswick, Maine. His classmates included poet Henry Wadsworth Longfellow and future president Franklin Pierce.

After college, Hawthorne returned to Salem and his mother's house, where he began writing the stories that would become *Twice-Told Tales* (1837). He anonymously published a novel, *Fanshawe* (1828), which he later regretted, withdrawing it and destroying copies. For eight months in 1836 he lived in Boston and served as the editor of *American Magazine of Useful and Entertaining Knowledge*.

Hawthorne fell in love with Sophia Peabody in 1837. Seeking financial security so they might marry, he took a position in the Boston Custom House. He next joined the utopian community Brook Farm in West Roxbury, Massachusetts, thinking he and his bride might settle there. The Old Manse in Concord, Massachusetts, provided a more traditional home. On July 9, 1842, the Hawthornes were married. During their three-year tenancy in the Old Manse, Hawthorne wrote the stories that comprise his second collection, *Mosses from an Old Manse* (1846), and the Hawthornes' first child, Una, was born. Their Concord neighbors included Ralph Waldo Emerson and Henry David Thoreau.

Returning to Salem with his wife and child, Hawthorne spent three years working in the Salem Custom House. He then wrote the work that brought him literary celebrity, *The Scarlet Letter* (1850). Moving to Lenox, Massachusetts, Hawthorne published *The House of the Seven Gables* (1851), inspired by Salem, as well as another collection of short stories, *The Snow-Image* (1852). While in the Berkshires, he befriended his neighbor, Herman Melville. During this time, the Hawthorne family grew to include two more children, Julian and Rose.

With an established literary reputation, Hawthorne and his family returned to Concord, Massachusetts, purchasing a home, The Wayside. *The Blithedale Romance*, inspired by his time at Brook Farm, was published in 1852. That year, Franklin Pierce, running for president, asked Hawthorne to write his presidential biography. The resulting *Life of Franklin Pierce* is considered to have played a role in Pierce's election. Hawthorne was rewarded in 1853 with a diplomatic post as the American consul in Liverpool. After his post ended, the Hawthornes traveled to Italy, providing material for Hawthorne's final complete novel, *The Marble Faun* (1860).

Hawthorne died in 1864. He is considered to be among the United States' greatest novelists.

# QUOTATIONS

OF

*Nathaniel Hawthorne*

*A*ll sorts of persons, and every individual, has a place to fill in the world, and is important in some respects, whether he chooses to be so or not.
– *The American Notebooks*, 1836

*W*hat would a man do, if he were compelled to live always in the sultry heat of society, and could never bathe himself in cool solitude?
– *The American Notebooks*, 1836

*H*ow strange and mysterious is our love of sleep! Fond as we are of life, we are yet content to spend a third of its little space in what, so far as relates to our own consciousness, is a daily, or nightly, annihilation. We congratulate ourselves when we have slept soundly; as if it were a matter of rejoicing that thus much of time has been snatched from the sum total of our existence—that we are several steps nearer to our graves, without perceiving how we arrived thither, or gaining either knowledge or enjoyment on the way.
– "Nature of Sleep," *American Magazine of Useful and Entertaining Knowledge*, 1836

$\mathcal{Y}$ou tell me that you have met with troubles and changes. I know not what they may have been; but I can assure you that trouble is the next best thing to enjoyment, and that there is no fate in this world so horrible as to have no share in either its joys or sorrows. For the last ten years, I have not lived, but only dreamed about living.
– Letter to poet Henry Wadsworth Longfellow, Salem, June 4, 1837

$\mathcal{M}$oral,—that what we need for our happiness is often close at hand, if we knew but how to seek for it.
– *The American Notebooks*, 1837

$\mathcal{M}$oonlight is sculpture; sunlight is painting.
– *The American Notebooks*, 1838

$\mathcal{I}$ never, till now, had a friend who could give me repose; all have disturbed me; and whether for pleasure or pain, it was still disturbance. But peace overflows from your heart to mine.
– Letter to his fiancée, Sophia Peabody, Boston, April 17, 1839

*M*y heart longed to drink your thoughts and feelings, as a parched throat for cold water.
– Letter to Sophia Peabody, Boston, April 30, 1839

*I* do detest all offices—all, at least, that are held on a political tenure. And I want nothing to do with politicians—they are not men; they cease to be men, in becoming politicians. Their hearts wither away, and die out of their bodies.
– Letter to Sophia Peabody, Boston, March 15, 1840

*A*n engagement to write a story must in its nature be conditional; because stories grow like vegetables, and are not manufactured, like a pine table.
– Letter to friend George S. Hillard, editor of *Token*, Brook Farm, July 16, 1841

*I*t is wonderful what a difference the sunshine makes; it is like varnish, bringing out the hidden veins in a piece of rich wood.
– *The American Notebooks*, Brook Farm, October 18, 1841

*I*f thou wouldst know what heaven is, before
thou comest thither hand in hand with thy
husband, then retire into the depths of thine own
spirit, and thou wilt find it there among holy
thoughts and feelings.
– Letter to Sophia Peabody, Brook Farm, October 18, 1841

*B*ees are sometimes drowned in the honey
which they collect—so some writers lost in their
collected learning.
– *The American Notebooks*, 1842

*I*n moods of heavy despondency, one feels as if it
would be delightful to sink down in some quiet
spot, and lie there forever, letting the soil
gradually accumulate and form a little hillock
over us, and the grass and perhaps flowers gather
over it. At such times, death is too much of an
event to be wished for;—we have not spirits to
encounter it; but choose to pass out of existence
in this sluggish way.
– *The American Notebooks*, 1842

*H*ow sweet it was to draw near my own home, after having lived so long homeless in the world; for no man can know what home is, until, as he approaches it, he feels that a wife will meet him at the threshold.
– *The American Notebooks*, Concord, August 7, 1842

*I* never could compress my thoughts sufficiently to write, in a very spacious room.
– *The American Notebooks*, Concord, August 7, 1842

*L*ast evening there was the most beautiful moonlight that ever hallowed this earthly world; and when I went to bathe in the river, which was as calm as death, it seemed like plunging down into the sky.
– *The American Notebooks*, Concord, August 22, 1842

*T*his proves that all gloom is but a dream and a shadow, and that cheerfulness is the real truth. It requires many clouds, long brooding over us, to make us sad; but one gleam of sunshine always suffices to cheer up the landscape.
– *The American Notebooks*, Concord, August 30, 1842

There is so much want and wretchedness in the world, that we may safely take the word of any mortal, when they say that they need our assistance; and even should we be deceived, still the good to ourselves, resulting from a kind act, is worth more than the trifle by which we purchase it.
– *The American Notebooks*, Concord, August 30, 1842

Mr. Thorow is a keen and delicate observer of nature—a genuine observer, which, I suspect, is almost as rare a character as even an original poet; and Nature, in return for his love, seems to adopt him as her especial child, and shows him secrets which few others are allowed to witness.
– On Henry David Thoreau, *The American Notebooks*, Concord, September 1, 1842

I cannot endure to waste anything so precious as autumnal sunshine by staying in the house.
– *The American Notebooks*, October 10, 1842

*I*t is a pity that there is no period after which an author may be safe. Forever and ever, he is to be tried again and again, and by everybody who chooses to be his Judge; so that, even if he be honorably acquitted at every trial, his ghost must be in everlasting torment.
– Letter to Margaret Fuller, Concord, February 1, 1843

*O*h, how blest I should be, were there nothing to do! Then I would watch every inch and hair's breadth of the progress of the season; and not a leaf should put itself forth, in the vicinity of our old mansion, without my noting it.
– *The American Notebooks*, Concord, April 25, 1843

*W*e should grow old and wear out twice as fast, if there were no winters;—it is summer, and not winter, that steals away mortal life. Well; we get the value of what is taken from us.
– *The American Notebooks*, Concord, June 23, 1843

$\mathcal{T}$he infirmities, that come with old-age, are the interest on the debt of nature, which should have been more seasonably paid. Often, the interest is a heavier payment than the principal.

– *The American Notebooks*, 1845

$\mathcal{C}$hildless men, if they would know something of the bliss of paternity, should plant a seed,— be it squash, bean, Indian corn, or perhaps a mere flower or worthless weed,— should plant it with their own hands, and nurse it from infancy to maturity altogether by their own care. If there be not too many of them, each individual plant becomes an object of separate interest.

– "The Old Manse," *Mosses from an Old Manse*, 1846

$\mathcal{S}$peaking of summer squashes, I must say a word of their beautiful and varied forms. They presented an endless diversity of urns and vases, shallow or deep, scalloped or plain, moulded in patterns which a sculptor would do well to copy, since Art has never invented anything more graceful.

– "The Old Manse," *Mosses from an Old Manse*, 1846

*H*ouses of any antiquity in New England are so invariably possessed with spirits that the matter seems hardly worth alluding to.
– "The Old Manse," *Mosses from an Old Manse*, 1846

*S*o far as I am a man of really individual attributes I veil my face; nor am I, nor have I ever been, one of those supremely hospitable people who serve up their own hearts, delicately fried, with brain sauce, as a tidbit for their beloved public.
– "The Old Manse," *Mosses from an Old Manse*, 1846

*T*here is a kind of ludicrous unfitness in the idea of a time-stricken and grandfatherly lilac bush.
– "Buds and Bird Voices," *Mosses from an Old Manse*, 1846

$\mathcal{A}$pple-trees, on the other hand, grow old
without reproach. Let them live as long as they
may, and contort themselves into whatever
perversity of shape they please, and deck their
withered limbs with a springtime gaudiness of
pink blossoms; still they are respectable, even if
they afford us only an apple or two in season.
– "Buds and Bird Voices," *Mosses from an Old Manse*, 1846

*Nath. Hawthorne*

$\mathcal{B}$lessed are all simple emotions, be they dark
or bright! It is the lurid intermixture of the two
that produces the illuminating blaze of the
infernal regions.
– "Rappaccini's Daughter," *Mosses from an Old Manse*, 1846

*Nath. Hawthorne*

$\mathcal{I}$ think we are very happy—a truth that is not
always so evident to me, until I step aside from
our daily life. How I love thee!—how I love our
children! Can it be that we are really parents!
— that two beautiful lives have gushed out of our
life! I am now most sensible of the wonder, and
the mystery, and the happiness.
– Letter to his wife, Sophia Hawthorne, Salem, July 13, 1847

$W$ords—so innocent and powerless as they are, as standing in a dictionary, how potent for good and evil they become, in the hands of one who knows how to combine them!

– *The American Notebooks*, 1848

$H$uman nature will not flourish, any more than a potato, if it be planted and replanted, for too long a series of generations, in the same worn-out soil.

– "The Custom House," *The Scarlet Letter*, 1850

$I$t contributes greatly towards a man's moral and intellectual health, to be brought into habits of companionship with individuals unlike himself, who care little for his pursuits, and whose sphere and abilities he must go out of himself to appreciate.

– "The Custom House," *The Scarlet Letter*, 1850

*I*t is a good lesson—though it may often be a hard one—for a man who has dreamed of literary fame, and of making for himself a rank among the world's dignitaries by such means, to step aside out of the narrow circle in which his claims are recognized, and to find how utterly devoid of significance, beyond that circle, is all that he achieves, and all he aims at.

– "The Custom House," *The Scarlet Letter*, 1850

*M*oonlight, in a familiar room, falling so white upon the carpet, and showing all its figures so distinctly,—making every object so minutely visible, yet so unlike a morning or noontide visibility,—is a medium the most suitable for a romance-writer to get acquainted with his illusive guests.

– "The Custom House," *The Scarlet Letter*, 1850

*T*he page of life that was spread out before me seemed dull and commonplace, only because I had not fathomed its deeper import.

– "The Custom House," *The Scarlet Letter*, 1850

On the breast of her gown, in fine red cloth, surrounded with an elaborate embroidery and fantastic flourishes of gold thread, appeared the letter A.
– *The Scarlet Letter*, 1850

In our nature, however, there is a provision, alike marvellous and merciful, that the sufferer should never know the intensity of what he endures by its present torture, but chiefly by the pang that rankles after it.
– *The Scarlet Letter*, 1850

Trusting no man as his friend, he could not recognize his enemy when the latter actually appeared.
– *The Scarlet Letter*, 1850

It is to the credit of human nature, that, except where its selfishness is brought into play, it loves more readily than it hates.
– *The Scarlet Letter*, 1850

*L*et men tremble to win the hand of woman, unless they win along with it the utmost passion of her heart!
– *The Scarlet Letter*, 1850

*T*he scarlet letter was her passport into regions where other women dared not tread.
– *The Scarlet Letter*, 1850

*L*ove, whether newly born, or aroused from a death-like slumber, must always create a sunshine, filling the heart so full of radiance, that it overflows upon the outward world.
– *The Scarlet Letter*, 1850

*N*o man, for any considerable period, can wear one face to himself, and another to the multitude, without finally getting bewildered as to which may be the true.
– *The Scarlet Letter*, 1850

*I*t is singular, however, how long a time often passes before words embody things; and with what security two persons, who choose to avoid a certain subject, may approach its very verge, and retire without disturbing it.
– *The Scarlet Letter*, 1850

*I*t is a curious subject of observation and inquiry, whether hatred and love be not the same thing at bottom. Each, in its utmost development, supposes a high degree of intimacy and heart-knowledge; each renders one individual dependent for the food of his affections and spiritual life upon another; each leaves the passionate lover, or the no less passionate hater, forlorn and desolate by the withdrawal of his subject.
– *The Scarlet Letter*, 1850

*G*reat men have to be lifted upon the shoulders of the whole world, in order to conceive their great ideas, or perform their great deeds. That is, there must be an atmosphere of greatness round them;—a hero cannot be a hero, unless in a heroic world.

– *The American Notebooks*, May 7, 1850

*H*appiness, in this world, if it comes at all, comes incidentally. Make it the object of pursuit, and it leads us a wild-goose chase, and is never attained. Follow some other object, and very possibly we may find that we have caught happiness without dreaming of such luck; but, likely enough, it is gone the moment we say to ourselves—"Here it is!"—like the chest of gold that treasure-seekers find.

– *The American Notebooks*, 1851

*T*his book, if you would see anything in it, requires to be read in the clear, brown, twilight atmosphere in which it was written; if opened in the sunshine, it is apt to look exceedingly like a volume of blank pages.

– Preface to the third edition of *Twice-Told Tales*, Lenox,
  January 11, 1851

*H*alf-way down a by-street of one of our New England towns stands a rusty wooden house, with seven acutely peaked gables, facing towards various points of the compass, and a huge, clustered chimney in the midst. The street is Pyncheon Street; the house is the old Pyncheon House; and an elm-tree, of wide circumference, rooted before the door, is familiar to every town-born child by the title of the Pyncheon Elm.

– *The House of the Seven Gables*, 1851

There is something so massive, stable, and almost irresistibly imposing in the exterior presentment of established rank and great possessions, that their very existence seems to give them a right to exist; at least, so excellent a counterfeit of right, that few poor and humble men have moral force enough to question it, even in their secret minds.

– *The House of the Seven Gables*, 1851

In this republican country, amid the fluctuating waves of our social life, somebody is always at the drowning-point.

– *The House of the Seven Gables*, 1851

People in difficulty and distress, or in any manner at odds with the world, can endure a vast amount of harsh treatment, and perhaps be only the stronger for it; whereas they give way at once before the simplest expression of what they perceive to be genuine sympathy.

– *The House of the Seven Gables*, 1851

*I*t is very queer, but not the less true, that people are generally quite as vain, or even more so, of their deficiencies than of their available gifts.
– *The House of the Seven Gables*, 1851

*I*n cases of distasteful occupation, the second day is generally worse than the first; we return to the rack with all the soreness of the preceding torture in our limbs.
– *The House of the Seven Gables*, 1851

*W*hat an instrument is the human voice! How wonderfully responsive to every emotion of the human soul!
– *The House of the Seven Gables*, 1851

*P*ersons who have wandered, or been expelled, out of the common track of things, even were it for a better system, desire nothing so much as to be led back.
– *The House of the Seven Gables*, 1851

*M*an's own youth is the world's youth; at
least, he feels as if it were, and imagines that
the earth's granite substance is something not
yet hardened, and which he can mould into
whatever shape he likes.
– *The House of the Seven Gables*, 1851

*Nath¹ Hawthorne*

"*O*ur first youth is of no value; for we are
never conscious of it until after it is gone. But
sometimes— always, I suspect, unless one is
exceedingly unfortunate— there comes a sense
of second youth, gushing out of the heart's joy at
being in love; or, possibly, it may come to crown
some other grand festival in life, if any other such
there be."
– Mr. Holgrave to Phoebe Pyncheon, *The House of the Seven
   Gables*, 1851

*Nath¹ Hawthorne*

*T*hus it is that the grief of the passing moment
takes upon itself an individuality, and a character
of climax, which it is destined to lose after a
while, and to fade into the dark grey tissue

common to the grave or glad events of many years ago. It is but for a moment, comparatively, that anything looks strange or startling, — a truth that has the bitter and the sweet in it.
– *The House of the Seven Gables*, 1851

*M*en of his strength of purpose, and customary sagacity, if they chance to adopt a mistaken opinion in practical matters, so wedge it and fasten it among things known to be true, that to wrench it out of their minds is hardly less difficult than pulling up an oak.
– *The House of the Seven Gables*, 1851

"*B*ut I suppose I am like a Roxbury russet, — a great deal the better, the longer I can be kept."
– Old Uncle Venner, *The House of the Seven Gables*, 1851

*A*fter supper, I put Julian to bed; and Melville and I had a talk about time and eternity, things of this world and of the next, and books, and publishers, and all possible and impossible matters, that lasted pretty deep into the night; and if truth must be told, we smoked cigars even within the sacred precincts of the sitting-room.

– On Herman Melville, "Twenty Days with Julian & Little Bunny by Papa," *The American Notebooks*, Lenox, August 1, 1851

*M*ercy on me, was ever man before so be-pelted with a child's talk as I am! It is his desire of sympathy that lies at the bottom of the great heap of his babblement. He wants to enrich all his enjoyments by steeping them in the heart of some friend.

– On his five year-old son, "Twenty Days with Julian & Little Bunny by Papa," *The American Notebooks*, Lenox, August 10, 1851

*I* have before now experienced, that the best way to get a vivid impression and feeling of a landscape, is to sit down before it and read, or become otherwise absorbed in thought; for then, when your eyes happen to be attracted to the landscape, you seem to catch Nature at unawares, and see her before she has time to change her aspect. The effect lasts but for a single instant, and passes away almost as soon as you are conscious of it; but it is real, for that moment.

– "Twenty Days with Julian & Little Bunny by Papa," *The American Notebooks*, Lenox, August 16, 1851

*In* youth, men are apt to write more wisely than they really know or feel; and the remainder of life may be not idly spent in realizing and convincing themselves of the wisdom which they uttered long ago.

– Preface, *The Snow-Image and Other Tales*, Lenox, November 1, 1851

*The* greatest obstacle to being heroic is the doubt whether one may not be going to prove one's self a fool; the truest heroism is to resist the doubt; and the profoundest wisdom to know when it ought to be resisted, and when to be obeyed.

– *The Blithedale Romance*, 1852

"Death should take me while I am in the mood."
– Miles Coverdale, *The Blithedale Romance*, 1852

Destiny, it may be, — the most skilful of stage-managers, — seldom chooses to arrange its scenes, and carry forward its drama, without securing the presence of at least one calm observer.
– *The Blithedale Romance*, 1852

No sagacious man will long retain his sagacity, if he live exclusively among reformers and progressive people, without periodically returning into the settled system of things, to correct himself by a new observation from that old stand-point.
– *The Blithedale Romance*, 1852

"No summer ever came back, and no two summers ever were alike," said I, with a degree of Orphic wisdom that astonished myself.
– Miles Coverdale to Priscilla, *The Blithedale Romance*, 1852

*B*ut a man cannot always decide for himself whether his own heart is cold or warm.
– *The Blithedale Romance*, 1852

*C*aresses, expression of one sort or another, are necessary to the life of the affections, as leaves are to the life of a tree. If they are wholly restrained, love will die at the roots.
– *The American Notebooks*, 1853

*R*omance and poetry, ivy, lichens, and wall-flowers, need ruin to make them grow.
– Preface, *The Marble Faun*, 1860

*F*or nobody has any conscience about adding to the improbabilities of a marvellous tale.
– *The Marble Faun*, 1860

"*T*ime flies over us, but leaves its shadow behind."
– Donatello, Count of Monte Beni, *The Marble Faun*, 1860

"*N*obody, I think, ought to read poetry, or look at pictures or statues, who cannot find a great deal more in them than the poet or artist has actually expressed."

– Hilda, *The Marble Faun*, 1860

*Y*our own life is as nothing, when compared with that immeasurable distance; but still you demand, none the less earnestly, a gleam of sunshine, instead of a speck of shadow, on the step or two that will bring you to your quiet rest.

– *The Marble Faun*, 1860

*B*ut in most hearts, there is an empty chamber, waiting for a guest.

– *Doctor Grimshawe's Secret*, an unfinished novel begun in 1860

*T*he author seems to imagine that he has compressed a great deal of meaning into these little, hard, dry pellets of aphoristic wisdom. We disagree with him.

– "Chiefly about War Matters by a Peaceable Man," *Atlantic Monthly*, July 1862

Nath'l Hawthorne